THE BEGINNER'S
Buying and Selling on

eBay

- 📷 Getting started
- 📷 Successful selling
- 📷 Finding bargains
- 📷 Bidding to win
- 📷 Payment methods
- 📷 Postage costs

CLARE McCANN

summersdale

THE BEGINNER'S GUIDE TO BUYING AND SELLING ON eBAY
Copyright © Clare McCann, 2006

All trademarks are acknowledged as belonging to their respective companies.

The right of Clare McCann to be identified as the author of this work has been
asserted in accordance with sections 77 and 78 of the Copyright, Designs and
Patents Act 1988.

Condition of Sale
This book is sold subject to the condition that it shall not, by way of trade
or otherwise, be lent, re-sold, hired out or otherwise circulated in any form
of binding or cover other than that in which it is published and without a
similar condition including this condition being imposed on the subsequent
publisher.

Summersdale Publishers Ltd
46 West Street
Chichester
West Sussex
PO19 1RP
UK

www.summersdale.com

Printed and bound in Great Britain

ISBN 1-84024-504-2
ISBN 978-1-84024-504-2

Warning and Disclaimer
Every effort has been made to make this book as accurate as possible. The authors
and publishers shall have neither responsibility nor liability to any person or
entity with respect to any loss or damage arising from information contained
within this book.

While every effort has been made to trace copyright holders, Summersdale
Publishers apologise in advance for any unintentional omission or neglect and
will be pleased to insert appropriate acknowledgement to companies or individuals
in any subsequent edition of this publication.

For my father John, who always knows
a good deal when he sees one

Contents

Introduction

In just over a decade, eBay has transformed itself from a niche collector's fair to a massive centre for global commerce. Now professional online retailers sell their goods on eBay alongside mums with second-hand baby clothes.

In the last year more than 50,000 Britons used eBay as a place to make a little extra cash or secure a bargain. My own introduction to eBay began with a two-year-old car with 48,000 miles on the clock. No garage would touch it with a barge pole and adverts in the press had generated no response. In desperation – and, I admit, with little hope of selling it – I put it on eBay. When the auction ended seven days later, and after some bargaining by e-mail, a lovely couple from East Sussex arrived at my house with £4,000 in cash.

Inspired by the success of this unlikely sale, I next turned my attentions to my £300 Ikea sofa which, though adequate, I wanted to replace with a sofabed. My premise was simple; if I could get someone to take it away, it was worth doing. If I could get someone to pay me and take it away, it was *really* worth doing! I started the auction at £20, hoping it might reach £70. A week later – after several increasingly over-excited phone calls from my sister ('It's gone up again!') – my 6-year-old sofa sold for £160. The new owners did a 150-mile trip in a borrowed van to collect it and I got a hassle-free transaction and a hefty deposit on the furniture to replace it.

It's easy to read these two accounts and wonder if the people involved were, to put it frankly, a little insane, but there are two sides to every sale on eBay. The couple who purchased my car had done their research and knew that that make of car was built to manage a high mileage, plus they only wanted it as a second car and so within a couple of years that high mileage would have averaged out to something more reasonable.

The pair who bought the sofa needed something to furnish a buy-to-let flat they owned. Even the cheapest settee they could buy new would have cost £100 more than the price they bid on mine, so in the end the saving was worthwhile to them.

Whilst one half of eBay activity consists of people happily exchanging the contents of their lofts and garages for cash, the other half involves lucky punters finding the kind of bargains you used to be forced to trawl car boot sales and the classifieds for.

Although I started as a seller on eBay, I quickly became a buyer. For years I'd been trying to track down *The Cosby Show* on DVD. I then found it, but it was only available to members of a movie club in America and to join the club you had to have an address in the United States. I thought I'd reached a dead end until I tried searching for it on eBay and found there was a thriving trade in second-hand copies of the discs.

Now I use eBay as the first port of call for everything I buy. Recently I've bought a second-hand North Face ski jacket which was £185 less than the retail price and a brand new pair of Nike trainers, one of several on sale at a Buy It Now price of £19.99 because they were last year's design.

eBay offers the chance to secure the kind of bargains you feel compelled to tell people about and to find a new home for the most extraordinary of possessions. Now the time has come to introduce you to a website that will (and I don't say this lightly!) change your life and your shopping habits forever. Have fun!

Facts & Figures

The most expensive item sold on the UK website was Lady Thatcher's handbag, which went for £103,000.

PART ONE: eBAY BASICS

How eBay Was Born

Founded just over a decade ago, eBay is the most popular shopping site on the Internet, but contrary to popular belief it wasn't founder Pierre Omidyar's wife's fascination with little plastic sweet dispensers that gave him the idea that was to turn him into one of America's richest men.

The myth that eBay was conceived when Pierre's fiancée (now wife) Pam Wesley remarked on the difficulty she was having finding opportunities to buy and sell Pez dispensers was in fact dreamed up by a publicist looking for a human story behind this massive Internet success. You can still find references to the Pez story all over the Internet, in books and even in eBay's official history on the site, but sadly at best it's a spin on the truth.

The fact is Pierre – an early Internet enthusiast – was looking for a gap in the market. He knew that people needed a simple way to buy and sell all kinds of items on a level playing field and to meet other users with similar interests. He wasn't a hobbiest who stumbled on a brilliant idea, but one of Silicon Valley's canniest entrepreneurs. By the time he came up with the idea for eBay, he was already a self-made millionaire, having sold his business eShop to Microsoft whilst still in his twenties.

Established initially as the American auction site ebay.com, eBay now operates in 33 countries and its founder is worth some $10.4 billion.

Facts & Figures

Over half of the UK's online population visits the eBay online marketplace at least once a month.

eBay Myths Exploded

I'm not technical – I don't think I could use eBay.
If you've got a computer, you are technical enough to use eBay! It wouldn't be as successful as it is if it wasn't very easy to use.

How does it work? Do you wait for the money before you send something?
Definitely! Once an item sells, the seller waits for payment and only when it's been received should the item be sent out.

What do you do with something that's too big to send in the post?
You list it choosing the 'Will arrange for local pickup only (no postage)' option. The winning

bidder will then either pay in advance of collection, so that funds can clear, or will pay in cash when they collect.

What happens if you pay for something and you never get it?

Two things. You can leave negative feedback so that anyone else who trades on eBay can see that you had problems with the seller; and in most cases you are protected by eBay, so they will refund any losses you have.

How do you find things?

It's just like an Internet search engine – you type in what you are looking for, hit return and eBay finds anything that matches.

How do people pay you?

By the usual old-fashioned methods like cheque or postal order, or most commonly by a simple electronic money transfer system called PayPal.

Weird & Wonderful eBay Sales

A 1926 Coca-Cola advertising sign sold on eBay for $2,650.

I'm not sure I have anything I could sell.

I am and I've never even met you! One person's trash is another person's treasure. You'll be astonished by what people buy. Start by clearing out the loft, the garage and your wardrobe.

Can I sell my car/table/CDs on eBay?

There are restrictions on what you can sell on eBay but most people won't be affected by them: most of the prohibited items are illegal to trade anywhere, so it's just a matter of exercising some common sense. But you can't sell your pet on eBay, just in case you were thinking of it.

Setting Up an eBay Account

The first thing you'll have to do before you start snapping up bargains on eBay is register. Registration is free and, providing you have the right information at hand, it is pretty straightforward.

Before you start make sure you have the following details handy:

- a credit or debit card
- your bank details
- your full home address including postcode
- an e-mail address you can access easily
- your phone number

Log on to www.ebay.co.uk. On the first page of eBay just above where it says 'Welcome To eBay', you'll see the note 'Sign in or register'. Click on 'register'. You then go through a few pages of form filling, where you'll need to provide your full name and contact information. Don't give any false information. If, for instance, your phone number turns out to be made up, eBay can suspend your account and cancel your auctions.

If your e-mail address is an 'anonymous' Internet one, like a Yahoo or Hotmail account, you'll need to provide a valid credit card number to verify your identity. Most sellers won't send goods to a buyer who doesn't have a confirmed e-mail address. eBay won't make a charge to your card; this process is simply to prove your identity and help prevent fraud. To avoid this process you can use an official e-mail address, such as one issued by your place of work or a paid-for Internet service provider.

During this process you'll be asked to choose a user ID and password. This is probably the most time-consuming part of the process! You can't use your e-mail address, anything obscene or something that is taken by another eBay user. Your user ID will be visible to all when you are buying or selling, so don't pick anything silly (PinkPants) or give yourself a name that might arouse suspicion (HonestJohn). It's better to have a boring name than something that stands out for all the wrong reasons.

You can change your user ID but, to avoid confusion, eBay only allows you to do so once in a 30-day period. Best just to get it right the first time!

You'll also be asked for a password: make it something that's easy for you to remember, as eBay asks for it quite frequently to prevent other people who may be using your computer from accessing sensitive areas of your account or bidding on an item without your consent (particularly important if you have children!).

Weird & Wonderful eBay Sales

Stuck for inspiration on what to sell on eBay? How about taking some inspiration from some of the more bizarre transactions that have taken place during the site's history.

Once you've completed all your information, eBay will send you an e-mail containing a link and instructions for confirming your registration. Doing this confirms for eBay that your e-mail account is valid and active.

At this stage you can choose to make your account a seller's account (or you can come back and do this at a later stage when you decide to start selling). To complete this process you'll have to provide eBay with some additional financial information, so you'll need your bank account details and a valid credit or debit card.

Providing this information will verify your seller's account and provide you with a facility to pay the fees you will incur when you sell an item. The basic cost of listing an item on eBay is 35p, but if your item sells you will be required to pay a percentage of the final price too (about £1 for an item that sells for £20).

If it seems like eBay is asking for a lot of information, you should rest assured that this is the process that every seller on the site has to go through and it enables eBay to make sure everyone is accountable for the goods they sell, thereby cutting down on fraud.

Don't panic, though, your information will be kept private on eBay's secure servers and your information won't be passed on to any third parties. However, buyers and sellers who are in the process of or have completed a transaction with you can request this information if they have a legitimate reason to have it (for instance if you haven't paid!).

Setting Up a PayPal Account

PayPal allows anyone with an e-mail address to buy and sell in most major currencies securely. It acts as a third party, handling the transfer of money between you and the person you are sending it to and prevents anyone you buy from or sell to seeing your bank details.

PayPal is the most popular method of payment for goods on eBay and is accepted on nine out of ten auctions. In fact, it's so popular that eBay actually bought PayPal out in 2004, so they are now under the same ownership. There are obvious advantages to this, the main one being that the two websites synchronise with each other perfectly. You can log on to www.ebay.co.uk and click a PayPal button to pay for an item and you can log on to www.paypal.com and click a button to see which successful eBay bids need paying for. Sometimes people who are new to online trading don't even realise they are different websites.

If you're going to make regular transactions on eBay, I can't stress just how vital having a PayPal account is. Not only will it make your payments easier (no writing and posting of cheques) but, because traders find it such a convenient way to receive payments, many will list this as the only method of payment they will accept. So although it might seem like a hassle now, it's worth spending some time doing a bit of extra form filling.

Facts & Figures

eBay has over 10 million registered users in the UK and 157 million worldwide.

To access the PayPal site either type www.paypal.com/uk/ directly into your browser, or click on the link that you'll find on the front page of ebay.co.uk. Once on the PayPal website you'll see a button to 'Sign Up Now!' on the front page. Click on this.

Account Type

At the beginning of the account sign-up process, you'll be asked to select the type of account you want. The Personal Account is free and is usually all you will need to have for the first few months of trading on eBay. When you begin to sell large quantities of things on eBay (believe me, you will!) you'll probably need to upgrade to a Premier Account which will let you receive debit and credit card payments for a small fee, but you can do that without much hassle at a later stage.

Personal Details

Fill this in carefully! If you buy something on eBay and pay through PayPal, your seller will use whatever you have on record here as your delivery address. Any mistakes now could result in delays or failed deliveries in the future. Be particularly careful with any drop-down boxes; it's easy to accidentally click on the wrong county. Someone I sold to had done this, the result being that I had a delivery address that was obviously wrong and spent a couple of days trying to get hold of him before I was able to send his goods. Taking a little care at this stage will help you avoid unnecessary delays (especially annoying if the item is a birthday present or similar!).

E-mail Address and Password

As tempting as it is, I would advise against using the same password for PayPal as you have on your eBay account. If anyone manages to hack your eBay account, (rare, but it does happen) chances are they will successfully hack your PayPal account too. If you're really stuck for inspiration, you'd be better off using your password backwards on PayPal than completely ignoring this piece of advice for fear of forgetting!

Security Section

After you've ticked the box to confirm you accept PayPal's terms and conditions, you'll be asked to complete a security section at the bottom of the page. This will involve copying a strange set of letters and numbers into a box. It's PayPal's way of helping to prevent illegal automated registrations (where fraudsters use computers to complete multiple account applications).

Activation E-mail

As with eBay, when you complete the registration process with PayPal, you'll be sent an e-mail with a link to click on in order to complete your registration process. This again verifies that your e-mail address is correct and active and that nobody is using your e-mail address without your consent. Once you've done this, your account is open and you're ready to start receiving payments. You'll need to provide details of a credit or debit card before you can pay for items.

Weird & Wonderful eBay Sales

A woman from Jette in Brussels offered her husband for rent via eBay for a period of four hours and 32 minutes. She claimed she wanted a night out away from him. Her husband eventually sold for £38.36.

Remember, PayPal will only ask you to verify your account by e-mail during this sign-up process. Ignore any other e-mails you receive later claiming to be from PayPal – they will almost certainly be fraudulent (find out more by reading about 'phishing' in the chapter on eBay Scams).

Verification

If you intend to spend or withdraw more than £500 during the course of a month from your PayPal account, you'll need to go through a further process of verification. Don't worry about doing this immediately, but you may find yourself returning to do it at a later point.

- When you do choose to verify your account, you'll need to do three things:

- Firstly add your account details and set up a direct debit mandate.

- Then PayPal will deposit two small amounts into your bank account (yes, you can keep them, but don't get excited; each one is usually less than 10p!). Once they are in your account, which usually takes between three and five days, take a note of the two figures then log in to PayPal and tell them what they are. This confirms your bank account details are real.

Finally PayPal issues you with a 4-digit PIN number and makes an automated phone call to you (you can choose to receive the call immediately or in five minutes if you need to sign off the Internet to free up your phone line). During the call you will be asked to tap in the PIN number. This confirms your phone number is genuine.

Feedback

After every auction on eBay the buyer and seller have the option of leaving feedback for each other about the transaction. This feedback contributes towards the other party's overall feedback score and the comments you leave can be viewed by anyone using the site as an example of the service they are likely to receive from that buyer/seller. The number you see in brackets after an eBay username indicates their feedback score. For example 'JohnBrown (23)' will have received positive feedback from at least 23 eBay members. The more feedback a member collects the more accurate the picture of their trading practices.

This is how the system works:

> **+1 point** to your feedback score for each **positive** rating and comment left for you.

> **0 points** to your feedback score for each **neutral** rating and comment left for you.

> **-1 point** to your feedback score for each **negative** rating and comment left for you.

In addition you'll receive a feedback star once you've had ten or more positive feedbacks. Ten positive feedbacks is regarded as a landmark point for any new eBayers. Until you reach this point there will be certain restrictions on your buying and selling activity, the most significant of which is that you will be prohibited from selling anything at a fixed 'Buy It Now' price.

Whether you are intending to sell to or buy from an eBay user (or you are just curious!) you can get an idea of their transaction history at any time by clicking on the number next to their username. You'll then be able to view a breakdown of positive, negative and neutral feedback that they have received from people they have bought from or sold to in the last month, six months and year.

You'll also be able to read the comments left by people they have bought from or sold to, as well as seeing what the item was. Sometimes it helps to be able to see a feedback comment in context. A comment like 'It didn't work' is more important if the item is a brand new DVD player than if it is a book about how to get a date with a supermodel!

Occasionally you will come across a member who instead of having a number after their username

Facts & Figures

You can't sell alcohol, lottery tickets, used underwear, food past its sell-by date, tobacco, guns, fireworks, human parts and remains, pets, drugs, lock-picking devices or most Nazi memorabilia on eBay.

will have the word 'private' in brackets. This means that this eBay user has chosen to hide feedback comments and their rating. However, they can't hide everything! If you click on the word 'private' you'll be able to see a breakdown of their feedback.

Anyone who chooses to make their feedback private has a reason. They're either trying to hide a large amount of negative feedback or they don't want people to see their trading history (this can be the case when someone is trying to sell an item on for a higher price than they bought it for). So approach members with private feedback with caution.

Leaving feedback is voluntary and can be done any time up to 90 days after an auction ends. So, as

Facts & Figures

The gender split of British eBay users is 57% male, 43% female.

frustrating as it may seem when you are trying to collect positive feedback, you can't force someone to leave it. All you can do is make sure you're doing the right thing by leaving feedback as soon as you are happy. Your transaction may seem of little consequence, but every experience benefits people who will buy from and sell to that eBay user in the future.

How to Leave Feedback

- Click on the 'My eBay' button at the top of any eBay page and sign in if you haven't already.

- Click on 'Feedback' on the left-hand side of the page under 'My Account'.

- Click on the 'Leave feedback' button.

- As a general rule most feedback that is left is positive. Try to be fair towards the other party. Taking a few days to make a payment or post a parcel generally doesn't warrant negative feedback. Most sellers on eBay are not businesses; they are people like you and me with jobs and busy lives, so cut them a little slack.

Things to consider when leaving feedback:

Buyers

- Was the seller's description of the item accurate?
- Did they answer any e-mails promptly?
- Did it arrive promptly or when they said it would?
- If there was a delay, did they keep you informed?

Sellers

- Did the purchaser pay quickly by one of the methods specified in the auction?
- Were there any problems after the purchaser received the goods – did they make any unreasonable demands?

There is much debate amongst eBay users about whether a buyer or seller should leave feedback first. Many sellers will leave feedback as soon as you have paid for your item, but there is an argument stating that because a seller's side of the transaction does not end when the payment has been made, only when the customer has said they are happy with the goods, a buyer should be the first to leave feedback.

Experienced sellers might tell you that it's best not to leave feedback first, just in case your trading partner is planning to leave you negative feedback – for instance, if the goods don't arrive, get damaged in the post, or he or she is unhappy with the condition of the item purchased. Why should you help boost their feedback score if they don't help to boost yours! Really, there's no right or wrong and if your ideas are too fixed about who should be the first to leave feedback all that happens is a stand off develops and no one gets any feedback. If

Weird & Wonderful eBay Sales

A West Bank settler attempted to sell advertising space on the side of a former British fortress for £20,000, guaranteeing the successful bidder international media exposure when the settlement was cleared as part of the Israeli road map.

you're happy with your side of the deal then leave feedback.

So, what kind of feedback do you leave? The most important thing is that it is factual and accurate. You may feel like you struggle to fill your 80 characters on the feedback form and find yourself slipping into clichés, but none of this matters. No one cares how clever and beautifully written your feedback is, just that you've left any at all.

Here are some examples of real feedback I've had on my account:

Buyers

- 'Delivery was good. Item as described, very pleased.'
- 'Lovely item, nicely packed and very quickly dispatched.'
- 'Received quickly through the post. Excellent service.'

Sellers

- 'Prompt payment – excellent in every regard!!!'
- 'Great eBayer! Fast payment! Recommended! Thanks!'
- 'Great communication. A pleasure to do business with.'

You'll find there are popular phrases that pop up in feedback comments left on eBay. Expect a few people to comment that you are 'A+++++' or '10/10'.

Remember, although it is possible to remove feedback once you've left it, it's far from easy. It takes several days whilst eBay deals with it via a procedure called 'Mutual Feedback Withdrawal' and even after both the buyer and seller have consented to have the feedback removed, only the positive or negative point is removed; the comments themselves will remain on both your records. There is also a time limit to request the start of the Mutual Feedback Withdrawal process. Members must ask to begin the process within 30 days of either person leaving feedback or within

90 days of the transaction end date, whichever is later.

It's simpler just to regard all feedback as permanent. I can't stress enough how important it is to make sure you only leave fair and factual comments. Don't type anything in haste – sleep on it: you can always do it tomorrow. And don't be tempted to make personal remarks about a trader, they are likely to reflect just as badly on you.

What to Do if You Receive Negative Feedback

Don't panic! Your first bit of negative feedback may seem like the end of the world, but it happens to everyone sooner or later. If you've only had your account for a short time and have quite a low feedback score, some people might advise you to scrap it and start again. You can do

Facts & Figures

eBay.co.uk was launched in 1999.

this, although you'll need a new e-mail address and it does rather make a mockery of the entire system.

Better to focus on getting some good feedback to counterbalance your negative. If you're new most people will understand that sometimes you make mistakes early on and once it's a few transactions or months behind you it will be less relevant. What really matters is your entire trading record, not what went wrong during one transaction.

Of course, the more positive feedback you accrue the higher your percentage of positive feedback will be. One negative in ten transactions will mean only

Facts & Figures

At any given time there are more than 55 million items on sale on the site with about 2.7 million of those listed on the British site.

a 90% positive feedback score whereas one negative amongst 2,000 positives actually shows up as 100% positive.

Remember, collecting positive feedback is not the point of eBay, selling your goods is. Most people won't hold one or two bits of negative feedback against you, especially if they can see what went wrong. You can help to put the negative feedback in context by adding your comments to it. To do this click on 'Reply to feedback received' which you'll find at the bottom of your feedback page, underneath all the comments you've received. The page will change, so that there is a 'Reply' button after every comment. Click 'Reply' after the feedback you want to reply to and add your follow-up.

Make your response factual and calm. Don't get angry and make personal remarks, just explain the situation.

An appropriate response to a negative that says:
> 'This took ages to arrive and wasn't what I was expecting. Avoid!'

might be:

> 'Sent this two days after auction ended, item was as described. Offered refund.'

and not:

> 'This guy's an idiot – he got exactly what he bid for, I offered a refund and he still negged me.'

Occasionally you may find someone gives you a malicious piece of negative feedback, either in response to some feedback you left them or as a cruel attempt to wreck your account. Again, don't worry about this too much. It may seem very unfair, but if you use the 'Reply to feedback' facility, most people will be able to see what went on.

When You Need to Leave Negative Feedback

Always try to resolve a problem by contacting the seller/buyer directly before leaving any feedback. However, if after a few days your efforts to resolve the problem don't bear any fruit don't be afraid to leave negative feedback.

Negative feedback is as vital as positive. Your action might prevent someone else getting involved with an untrustworthy dealer. As I've mentioned before it's important that feedback is factual and accurate and this is even more important when it comes to leaving negative feedback. You are, of course, limited to 80 characters, but use them wisely and try to put as much information in your comment as you can.

Aim for something like this:
> 'Auction ended 26/9. Did not pay or respond to any e-mails.'

and not:
> 'Idiot! Stop wasting everyone's time and pay up when you bid!'

Weird & Wonderful eBay Sales

One American auctioned his entire collection of 2,080 Nintendo games on eBay. The shipping costs alone were $450. The haul eventually went for over $9,000.

My eBay

'My eBay' should quickly become your most visited part of the eBay site. This is where you can keep track of items you want to bid on, view how your own auctions are going and access information about items you have sold. To access this part of the site, just click on 'My eBay' at the top of any page and sign in with your username and password when prompted. The first page you view in My eBay is a summary of all your activity (watching, buying and selling). eBay will display useful buying and selling reminders for you at the top of the page, prompting you with sentences like:

'I need to leave feedback for 1 item.'
or:
'I need to post 2 items.'

My Messages

Beneath your reminders, you'll see your messages. Don't get too excited about this. Nearly all of the messages will be from eBay and will often be duplicates of ones that have been sent direct to your own e-mail account. As I write I actually have 21 'new' messages on eBay but on closer inspection I've read them all before and many of them date back a month or more. The real use for this facility is if you discover your own e-mail account blocks eBay's communications (as is sometimes the case with overzealous spam filters) then it will save you from missing out on any enquiries from potential buyers.

Items I'm Watching

These are items you want to keep an eye on, but are not ready to bid on. To add something to this list, click on 'Watch this item in My eBay' on the auction page of the item when you find it.

I choose to watch many items, not just the ones I intend to bid on. I might watch an item similar to one I intend to sell to see how many bids it gets and the price it reaches. If I'm buying an item that a user sells regularly I'll watch a few sales of the object to see the average price it goes for, so I know how much I'll have to bid to win it. Occasionally I'll see someone asking far too much for a horrible item on eBay and out of curiosity I'll stick it on My eBay so I can find out if it ever sells!

Buying Totals

This provides you with a short summary of the number of items you are currently bidding on or winning, how many you have bought in the last month, and their total value.

Items I've Won

Here you'll be able to see the items you've won recently at auction, how much you paid for them, when the auction finished and whether you or the seller has left feedback. You'll find this section useful if you make a purchase from a seller and decide you want to buy another item from them. If you want to do this click on the seller's username: this will take you to their feedback page and from there you'll be able to see a link to 'Items For Sale' on the top right-hand side of the page.

Items I Didn't Win

This section shows you a list of items you have bid on but lost to a higher bidder.

Selling Totals

As with Buying Totals, this shows you a short summary of the number of items you are selling, the quantity of bids you've had and the total value they eventually sell for. You can also see the total value of all the sales you have made in the last 60 days. It's great fun seeing how much money eBay has made you!

Items I've Sold

If you intend to become a prolific seller on eBay this easy-to-view part of My eBay will prove essential when you're trying to organise sending out your items. The section allows you to see at a glimpse who has paid for their item and – if you click on the box to verify it – which items have been dispatched. You can also get a buyer's address from here. Just click on the total price next to the item they have bought.

On the left-hand side of this main page of My eBay you can also access further pages which will show you useful things like favourite searches, sellers and categories, as well as information about your account, links to the 'Dispute Console' (the section of the site you visit if you have problems with a transaction) and access to your PayPal account. Go explore! You can always click on the 'Back' button on your browser to return to where you started.

Facts & Figures

A CD sells every 11 seconds, a toy car every 35 seconds, every minute a mobile phone is bought and every two minutes a car, laptop and teddy bear are snapped up by eBay bidders.

PART 2: BUYING

What to Buy on eBay

The most commonly searched-for word on eBay is 'new', which shatters the popular misconception that most things that are sold on eBay are second-hand.

I now use eBay as my first port of call for anything I am considering buying. A quick search may save you money or find you a quicker delivery than other online retailers might offer.

But be careful not to make the mistake that many newbies do in assuming that everything on eBay is a bargain! It pays to search the web for new items to make sure you are getting the best price. Some sellers take advantage of the assumption that everything on eBay is cheap and buy in stock from elsewhere on the Net to sell in an eBay auction at a profit.

One thing that is well worth buying on eBay is anything that is out of season. You can pick up items very cheaply by purchasing them at the wrong time of year. Christmas items in the summer, golf shorts in the winter – you get the idea.

Weird & Wonderful eBay Sales

A 1999 Volkswagen Golf became an unlikely gold mine for one 21-year-old when its previous owner was elected pope. Benjamin Habe bought the car, once owned by Pope Benedict XVI, for 10,000 Euros and sold it four months later for 188,938 Euros.

How to Find What You Want

There are two ways of starting your search on eBay. Let's imagine you are looking for a black skirt: you can either search all auctions to find those featuring the words 'black' and 'skirt' or you could just look in the women's clothing category.

To try the search method, type your keyword(s) into the box you will find at the top right of every page on eBay. You'll see the words 'Start new search' written in the box; when you click in it the words will disappear and you can replace them with your own words. Now click the 'Search' button and eBay will trawl all its categories to find auctions that match your search criteria.

Choose your search words carefully and try alternatives. If you're looking for a boy's fleece, try not just 'boy's fleece' but also 'children's fleece', 'kid's fleece', 'child's fleece' as well as variations on the theme with incorrect punctuation or spelling, such as 'kids fleece' or 'boy's fleace'. Many great bargains on eBay are found by people who search for misspellings!

Often the number of results can be very high (a search for 'black skirt' produces an average of

Weird & Wonderful eBay Sales

A Nevada woman, Molly Demers, auctioned the back of her head as advertising space on eBay. Online casino company GoldenPalace.com paid $18,000 for the woman to shave her head and have the company's name permanently tattooed on her bare cranium. Miss Demers agreed to sport the brand on the back of her head for a year before she regrew her locks.

10,000 results on the UK site alone), so to help you find what you are looking for, on the left-hand side of the page you'll be able to see a breakdown of the categories that the search results are in and decide to view just one of these categories (e.g. 'maternity clothing', 'women's clothing', 'vintage clothing', 'baby clothing').

This method of searching eBay will only check auction titles to see if they match your keywords. To carry out a more in-depth search of auction

Facts & Figures

It's not just second-hand CDs and positive feedback that's exchanged on eBay. Several pairs of trading partners have found they have more than an auction number in common and have met and married after meeting on the site.

descriptions as well as titles, tick the 'search title **and** description' box which you will find at the top of your results page just under the box which displays your keywords. Remember to click the 'Search' button again to see these additional results.

The second way to find auctions on eBay is to view all the auctions in a specific category.

To do this first click on the word 'Buy' which you will see at the top of any page on the eBay website. This page will show you all the main categories on eBay. Clicking on a main category will show you subcategories within it. So, for instance, clicking on 'Clothes, Shoes, Accessories' will show you an astonishing array of separate categories ranging from 'Corsets' to 'Flip-Flops'. Click on any of these and you will be able to see everything listed in it.

Whichever way you choose to access the list of auctions, the default setting will sort auctions by those that are ending soonest, meaning that the auctions that appear at the top of the list are those with the shortest period of time left to run. You can change this to view auctions by any of the following preferences:

Time: newly listed
Time: ending today
Time: new today
Price: lowest first
Price: highest first
Distance: nearest first
Condition: new first
Condition: used first
Payment: PayPal first
Payment: Paypal last

Facts & Figures

In August 2005, fashion jewellery retailer Pugster Inc. became the first eBay top seller to reach an eBay feedback score of 1,000,000.

Auction Page

Every item for sale on eBay has its own auction page. On this page is a wealth of information about the item and the seller. It's important you read it all through to avoid being caught out.

Here are the things you need to look for on the auction page.

Seller Information

On the top right-hand part of every auction page is a box which displays information about the seller. The crucial points to take note of here are the seller's feedback score (the number after their username) and the percentage of positive feedback. Beware of sellers with a single figure feedback score who are selling high value items. Generally the higher the score, the longer someone will have been trading on eBay. It is advisable to look for a seller with a positive feedback rating of 97% or higher. If you're concerned about their rating, click on 'Read feedback comments' to learn more about other people's experiences of trading with them.

Postage

To the left of the seller information is a brief summary of the main points of the auction. It's important to check the seller will send the item to your country, if based abroad, and indeed if they will send it at all.

Bear in mind that the price you will have to pay if you win an auction will be the amount you

Facts & Figures

There are an estimated 200 fraudulent auctions every day on eBay.

bid PLUS postage. Postage will be specified in the auction details, and never assume it will be reasonable – sellers can charge more or less anything they like!

As I have mentioned already, some things sold on eBay won't be sent to you at all. These will be listed as 'Will arrange for local pickup only (no postage)'. If this is the case take note of the item location just above the postage information. That's where the seller is based and the most likely location you'll be required to collect from. Occasionally a seller may be based in one location and an item in another – if so they should provide you with that information in the listing.

It's worth mentioning that if something is listed as a 'Buyer collect' item and seems to be of a size that could be posted, there's no harm in e-mailing the seller to ask if they will mail it. Sometimes (and I have been guilty of this!) sellers are only motivated to check the postage costs for an item once a potential buyer has made an appearance.

Auction Duration

In the central block of information at the top of the auction page, you can also find out details about an auction's duration. The listing will tell you the total auction duration, how long it has left to run and precisely when it will finish.

Payment Methods

Every seller will specify the payment methods they accept. Make sure you look at this before you bid – you'll find information about the payment methods that are accepted in this auction at the bottom of the page, just beneath the auction description. Be aware that some sellers don't accept PayPal payments, which can mean a delay in sending out your item while they wait for a cheque to clear. If you need something quickly this may influence whether you decide to bid in this auction or not.

Description

Read it thoroughly. If any information about the item isn't included, don't make assumptions. Use the 'Ask seller a question' feature at the top of the auction page. You'll find the link in the seller information box on the right-hand side of the page.

Seller's Payment Instructions

Read them and make sure you can comply BEFORE you bid. How quickly do they want payment? Are there any special conditions attached to this auction?

Weird & Wonderful eBay Sales

Stephen King, John Grisham and Amy Tan were among 16 authors who auctioned character roles in future books on eBay for charity. The auctioned raised $90,000 for The First Amendment Project.

Bidding

How and When to Bid

So you've found that rare movie poster or gorgeous vintage brooch and you're dying to place a bid and stake a claim on it! Before you bid on anything on eBay you need to consider two important things:

- The maximum you are willing to pay for the item
- How long the auction has left to run

Let's deal with the cost issue first. Often you'll find something on eBay being advertised at a bargain price and it's easy to assume you will win it for that price. However, auctions rarely end at the starting price.

You'll notice that people will bid on desirable items several days before the auction ends. The only person who really gains from this is the seller as early bidding will often force the price up as several potential buyers compete with each other to remain the winning bidder.

If you really want to win an auction you're going to have to sweat it out and wait until the last minute (and I really do mean last minute) to place your bid. The tried and tested way to win an auction on eBay is to follow these three rules:

- Bid once

- Bid the maximum you are willing to pay for an item

- Bid near the end of the auction

Let's tackle each of those key things one by one.

Bidding Once

eBay has a system called proxy bidding. What this means is that eBay will bid incrementally and competitively on your behalf up to your maximum, the amount of each increment depending on the current price of the item in question. So, whilst you can bid 55p for an item that is currently selling for 50p, you would not be able to bid £740.05 for an item that had reached £740; instead, where the latter is concerned, the next available bid would be £760.

The chart below shows you how the increments are determined.

Current price	Bid increment
£0.01–£1.00	£0.05
£1.01–£5.00	£0.20
£5.01–£15.00	£0.50
£15.01–£60.00	£1.00
£60.01–£150.00	£2.00
£150.01–£300.00	£5.00
£300.01–£600.00	£10.00
£600.01–£1,500.00	£20.00
£1,500.01–£3,000.00	£50.00
£3,000.01 and up	£100.00

This is how it works:

You see a CD by your favourite artist available for auction at an opening bid of 99p, but you would be happy to pay anything up to £10 for it. Instead of just bidding 99p, you bid £10.

eBay registers your bid and makes you the highest bidder at 99p. After you have done this another person comes along and bids £1.04 for the CD. In order to ensure you are still the winning bidder, eBay ups your bid to £1.24 and the interloper is told by eBay that they have been outbid. If they try again at £1.44 eBay will up your bid again to £1.64 to keep you as the winning bidder. This process will keep happening until a rival bidder exceeds your maximum bid of £10.

Don't worry that by using this process you might be giving away secret information about how

Weird & Wonderful eBay Sales

A Kent man attempted to sell his own kidney on eBay with a reserve price of £50,000, but the auction was promptly removed from the site.

much you are willing to pay for an item. No one other than the bit of software that does the bidding knows what your maximum is; the rival bidders don't know and neither does the person auctioning the item.

You won't end up paying more for your item by doing this, but you will save a lot of time logging back onto eBay every time you receive an e-mail from them saying you have been outbid. You are also far more likely to win the auction using this process.

Your Maximum

If you've already flicked through this book to the Dictionary of eBay Terms and Acronyms, you will have seen mention of 'Buyer's remorse': this is a phrase used to describe the regret a buyer feels when he or she gets carried away and bids far too much for an item.

It is extremely easy to get caught up in the excitement of an eBay auction and if you've been watching an item for several days you can develop a feeling of entitlement to it. The dress you are watching ceases to be just item '26554237' and becomes part of your wardrobe. You start to imagine the shoes you might wear with it and wonder whether it will reach you in time for the party you are going to at the weekend.

This is dangerous territory! Almost everything that has ever been on eBay will be on eBay again at a later point. This is why the site is so amazing. Those rare and hard to find things do pop up more than once!

With that in mind, be sensible in your bidding and consider carefully how much you are willing to pay for an item.

The price you decide on should be determined by three factors:

The total cost of the item. Some auctions on eBay look like incredible bargains until you see how

Facts & Figures

More than $1,381 (£786) worth of goods are traded on the site every second.

much the seller is charging for p. & p. An auction price of 99p with £10 p. & p. is not unheard of. Make sure you have accounted for how much you will have to pay for postage before you bid on an auction.

How many similar items are there? You might be willing to pay up to £80 for an item but if there are six of them available you probably don't need to bid that much until you've got down to the last of the six. Remember, if you've been keeping an eye on an auction via My eBay for a few days, do another search of the site to check that there aren't more recent auctions selling the same thing at a cheaper price – you might be surprised!

How much is it worth to you? It's an obvious thing to say, but certain things on eBay will be worth more to you than to other people, so you may be prepared to pay a bit extra to secure them.

Taking these three factors into consideration, decide on the maximum that you will be willing to pay for the item and then STICK TO IT! If you lose the auction because the price goes higher, don't feel frustrated: remember, it went for more than you were willing to pay for it.

One other thing to mention about the sum you decide to bid. Most people tend to think about sums of money in round numbers. You might decide you'd be happy to pay £20, £50 or £100 for an item and choose that as your maximum bid, but bidding a round figure will increase your chances of either tying with a previous bid or being outbid by a more experienced bidder whose highest bid is only a few pence more than yours. It's advisable, therefore, to always bid a few pence more than your maximum to increase your chances of winning. In my own experience, as rival bidders begin to place their bids in the final few minutes of an auction, many lose out by bidding £10 when my proxy bid was for £10.01.

Weird & Wonderful eBay Sales

Rosie Reid, the 19-year-old British student who offered her virginity for sale in an attempt to pay for her education, found her auction swiftly curtailed by eBay, but later set up her own website to complete the £8,000 transaction with a middle-aged businessman.

The End of the Auction

As you start to use eBay more and more, you'll probably discuss ideas about how to use it with fellow buyers and one thing you will often hear people suggesting is that the *only* way to guarantee becoming the winning bidder in an auction is to bid within the last minute of the auction. This is a practice known as 'sniping'. Sniping is perfectly legal on eBay, but you will find a few disgruntled users moaning about it in the forums because they think it's not fair. Ignore them – it's just sour grapes!

Sniping can work for you, but it has its disadvantages. Firstly if you have a slow Internet connection you may miss out because you're still clicking buttons and waiting for pages to load when the auction ends. Secondly if you wait until the very last minute and then your bid isn't high enough, there is no time to go back and make a higher bid.

My advice is to bid within the last ten minutes of an auction and the last five minutes if you are confident about the speed of your Internet connection and computer.

Paying

When you win an auction on eBay you will have to make payment by one of the methods specified by the seller. You'll be able to see what these are by reading the details of the auction or by looking at the invoice that your seller will e-mail you.

The golden rule with all payments that are made on eBay is to use only eBay's approved methods of payment. Sometimes this doesn't sink in with beginners, so I'm going to say it again…

ONLY EVER USE eBAY'S APPROVED METHODS OF PAYMENT

If you deviate from this one important rule you stand a high chance of becoming a statistic of fraud. I know one man who was persuaded to accept payment through a website that his buyer recommended, but that he had never heard of. The buyer made the payment, it appeared as if the payment had cleared on the website so the man handed over his £1,000 laptop and the website disappeared the next day. Another girl bought expensive concert tickets and sent the payment via Western Union. Several days passed and she still hadn't received the tickets: she tried to contact the seller and found they were no longer a registered user.

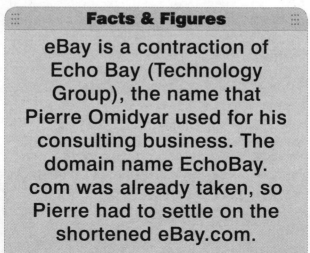

Facts & Figures

eBay is a contraction of Echo Bay (Technology Group), the name that Pierre Omidyar used for his consulting business. The domain name EchoBay. com was already taken, so Pierre had to settle on the shortened eBay.com.

As a double whammy, not only are you more likely to be a victim of a scam if you use a different payment service, but if you do, you won't be protected by eBay's fraud protection.

For more information about this and other cons to be aware of, read the chapter called 'Scams'.

Payments made by the following methods are approved by eBay and covered by their Standard Purchase Protection Programme which, in the event that you do not receive the item or that the item you receive is significantly different to the description, will reimburse the buyer up to £105 (£120 less £15 costs).

PayPal

This is a hugely popular payment method that allows you to send and receive money online in a variety of currencies using funds from your bank account, debit card, credit card or PayPal balance. In addition to eBay's Standard Purchase Protection Programme, paying by this method can cover you for up to £500. This makes PayPal the safest method of paying for high value items.

Personal Cheque

This is the second most popular method of payment after PayPal. If you pay by this method, expect the seller to delay posting your item until the cheque has cleared, which could be up to ten days.

Credit Cards

Most credit card issuers offer online protection and, should they refuse your claim, eBay's Standard Purchase Protection Programme should cover you. Be aware, though, that debit card users sometimes have much less protection.

In addition, although the following methods *aren't* recommended by eBay or covered by their Standard Purchase Protection Programme, there

Weird & Wonderful eBay Sales

One exasperated American father sold his children's Christmas presents on eBay after his children were naughty. The Nintendo Game Boy consoles sold for $3,000 – roughly 25 times what he would have paid for them.

are occasional circumstances where you may decide to use them. Generally the higher the sum you are dealing with the more wary you should be of using any of the following.

Escrow

Payment is held by the escrow service until you receive and approve the item. eBay warns people to exercise caution when using an escrow service and to only use www.escrow.com (US and UK).

Postal Orders

Postal Orders can be bought (for a small charge) and redeemed at post offices in the UK and are often used by people who don't have bank accounts in order to send money through the post. They are also a slightly faster alternative to sending a cheque, as they can be cashed immediately, with no need to be cleared by a bank.

Cash

The big down side to this method is that there is no way to prove payment was made. For this reason, eBay says that a seller is not allowed to insist that you pay by cash. However, in situations where you are collecting the goods you have bought, this is the payment method that many people find most practical. Always ask for a receipt and take the goods when you pay.

Bank Deposit

Many sellers swear by this method but eBay does not recommend it, saying that payments are difficult to trace or recover and that there are risks associated with the sharing of bank details. PayPal essentially does the same thing, with less risk, but it costs many sellers (though not all, depending on type of account) a small fee.

Facts & Figures

According to a recent survey British eBay users boost their income by an impressive average of £3,000 a year.

Banker's Draft

Commonly used to pay for large items like cars, this is a secure way for sellers to receive money from someone they don't know. Banker's drafts are essentially cheques made out by a bank rather than an individual and are far less likely to bounce.

Resolving Problems

With all private sales, not just those on eBay, it is important to remember the dictum '*caveat emptor*' (let the buyer beware). It is the buyer who bears the responsibility of checking that the goods they are about to purchase are of a condition that they are happy with: many of the so-called 'problems'

Facts & Figures

The UK is now eBay's third biggest market after the US and Germany.

that occur on eBay are actually the result of the buyer doing too little research.

It is extremely important that you carry out research on an item before you bid. If it's a high value item like a car or a computer, ask the seller if you can inspect it before you bid. Most will be accommodating; those who aren't generally have something to hide. Don't assume anything: there is a facility for asking sellers questions about their auctions – use it!

Here are some examples of common problems that arise after an eBay transaction; importantly not all are the fault of the seller:

Problems the seller isn't responsible for

- The buyer bidding too much for an item and then discovering it's not worth what they've bid – it's up to you to do the research on an item before you bid
- A problem with the item that the buyer discovers after they buy it and which the seller did not know about

- The buyer finding out an item is different to their expectations although they didn't confirm the accuracy of their expectations before bidding, e.g. it is older than you were expecting, but you never asked its age
- The buyer changing their mind about wanting something (remember, a bid on eBay is a legal contract)

These are not problems with a transaction but rather symptoms of buyer's remorse (mentioned previously). Any feelings of dissatisfaction arising from the above circumstances are because the buyer knows that however useless or clapped out the item they bought, no one forced them to bid on it!

Problems the seller is responsible for

- Inaccurate or false information included in the auction
- Items not being sent or being sent very late

If you have a problem with a purchase that you have made and you believe that problem is the responsibility of the seller, you can take one of the measures suggested below to try to resolve the matter. Note that starting a procedure through eBay is a last resort.

- Contact the seller and explain your problem.

- Seek the advice of other eBay users on the message boards. Click on 'Community' at the top of any page on the site.

- Open an 'Item Not Received' or 'Significantly Not as Described' dispute through eBay. To do this click on 'Help' at the top of any page and type 'dispute' into the 'Search Help' box.

Most problems can be solved without opening a dispute, but if you exhaust all other options and do need to do this, the procedure will work in the following way.

Weird & Wonderful eBay Sales

The football David Beckham ballooned over the bar in England's Euro 2004 quarter-final against Portugal fetched £18,700.

eBay contacts the seller to inform them that an Item Not Received or Significantly Not as Described dispute has been opened against them. Often, as with starting legal action, the start of this process is enough to conclude it.

The seller responds via eBay, volunteering either to discuss the problem with the buyer, refund what you paid or send a replacement.

Buyer and seller communicate via eBay's online process to try and resolve the problem.

At the end of this process, the dispute is resolved or the buyer can choose to file a claim under eBay's Standard Purchase Protection Programme, where they may be reimbursed up to £120 (minus a £15 processing cost).

PART THREE: SELLING

Getting Ready to Sell on eBay

Remember, if you didn't fill in the forms to make your account a seller's account during your initial registration, you'll need to do this as part of the selling process. In this case, the first thing eBay will ask you to do is provide some additional information including your card details and bank name, address and postcode.

To get going, click on 'Sell' at the top of any page. As a newbie you can only sell an item in an auction. Once you've got ten positive feedbacks you'll have the option to choose either to sell at auction or list as a 'Buy It Now'.

There are a few pages to navigate in order to complete the listing process.

Picking the Main Category

The first thing you will have to do is select the main category to list your item in. Don't worry about details here, this is just the top category – for instance, look for 'DVD, Film & TV', not 'Comedy DVDs'; you get to choose that more precise category later.

Picking the Subcategory

Next you have to select the first subcategory for your item, e.g. 'DVDs', then the next subcategory, e.g. 'TV Programmes', and the next, e.g. 'TV Comedy/Sitcom', until you have chosen a precise category for your item. In this case:

Facts & Figures

About 10,000 Britons have given up their jobs to take up trading online full time.

DVD, Film and TV > DVDs > TV Programmes > TV Comedy/Sitcom

Some items will have fewer subcategories, some will have more.

On this page you can also opt to list your auction in another category. You might want to use this if, for instance, you are selling children's clothes that are suitable for both sexes. You would list them first under 'Boys' Clothing' and you would add a second category of 'Girls' Clothing'. The catch is if you do this all your listing costs will be doubled. (The basic listing fee is 35p, but you can choose from a range of listing extras at an additional cost. You'll find more details in the 'Extra Features' chapter of this book.)

Facts & Figures

Pierre Omidyar sold his first item on eBay in 1995: a broken laser pointer that went for $14.

If you are confused about which category your item belongs in, do a search of the site using relevant keywords first and see if you can find a similar item. At the top of the auction page you'll be able to see a breakdown of the category information. It will look something like this:

Books, Comics & Magazines > Comics > US Comics > 1938–1955

If you are listing a CD, video or DVD, there'll be an additional step in the listing process which is designed to make listing these items easier. When you click 'Continue' you will be taken to a page that asks for the item's EAN number, more commonly known as the barcode number. If you type it in eBay will make standard information about this title available on the listing. Potential buyers will be able to read a description and review of the item without any further input from you.

Pictures and Item Details

The next page asks you to choose your price. Here you can add not just a starting price, but a reserve and a Buy It Now price should you want to.

eBay has also recently introduced a feature that allows you to donate a percentage of your sale to charity. There's an impressive selection to choose from and you can choose how much you want to give in a pull-down box.

Next you can choose the duration of your auction, add photographs (the first one is free) and choose which optional extras you want.

Right at the bottom of the page you even get a choice of visitor counters. Visitor counters – just above the 'Postage, payment details and return policy' box – do give potential purchasers some idea of your item's popularity and therefore the

Weird & Wonderful eBay Sales

Scottish laird Allan Macpherson-Fletcher was devastated when his £10,000 collection of eighteenth and nineteenth century porcelain was snatched from his mansion near Kingussie, in Invernesshire, but he recovered the lot when, a few days later, the burglars put the goods on eBay for auction.

chance that they'll have of securing your item for a reasonable price, so that's something you might want to consider when you choose whether to have one or not.

Payment and Postage

When it comes to choosing payment methods, the more you add the more you open up your potential audience. The same applies when it comes to ticking your 'post-to locations', so don't limit yourself too much.

If you are sending an item that you don't expect to sell for more than £28, you can insure it with a free Certificate of Posting, so select the pull-down box under postal insurance that says 'Included in P&P'.

On this page you can also specify a returns policy if you wish and include some payment instructions. Payment instructions are useful if you need an item to be paid for or collected by a certain date. I once waited two and a half months for one buyer to collect a surfboard he'd bought from my garage. He'd paid but was clearly rather enjoying the free storage I'd inadvertently offered him! Remember, what might seem obvious to you isn't obvious to potential buyers unless you point it out clearly in the text in your auction.

Review and Submit Listing

This is your final chance to look over everything you have put in the auction before you click on the 'submit listing' button at the bottom of the page.

You may click the 'Submit' button and then realise you have made an error on your listing – don't worry, all is not lost, even if several days have passed.

- Click on 'My eBay'

- From the menu on the left-hand side, select 'Selling' under 'All Selling'

- Select the item you want to alter by clicking on its auction title

- Click on 'Revise your item'

- Choose from the 'Edit' options displayed in blue text on the right-hand side of each category

Make your changes

Click on 'Save changes' at the bottom of the page

Click on 'Submit revisions' at the bottom of the main edit page

If there is under 12 hours to run on your auction or you already have a bid, you will not be allowed to edit your auction. Instead you are allowed to add additional information, which may, of course, be a line from you telling potential buyers about an error in the listing if you wish.

Facts & Figures

PayPal has more than 71 million member accounts worldwide.

What Sells on eBay

The easiest way to find out what sells successfully
on eBay is to search for the item you plan to sell
and see if there is one already being auctioned.
Take note not just of the price it has reached
but how many bids it has had and how long the
auction has left to run. An item being sold for
£100 may look encouraging, but if it has no bids
and the auction is nearing its end, the price may

Facts & Figures

There are 3,500
collectable
categories on eBay.

only reflect what the seller thinks it is worth and not what buyers are willing to pay.

Remember, you can choose to 'watch' an auction and in this way find out the final price it reaches. To do this click 'Watch this item', which is on the auction page on the right-hand side under the title. Then to monitor an auction's progress, just click on 'My eBay' at the top of any page.

There are some strange contradictions with regards to what sells on eBay. Here are a few examples:

Worth Selling

- Brand new current chart CDs (can sometimes sell for more than you bought them for!)
- Second-hand clothing from well-known and popular brands like Boden, Jigsaw or Monsoon
- New technology like iPods
- Second-hand Ikea furniture
- Anything that helps people sell on eBay, like mannequins or packaging
- Unusual, unique or collectable items
- Anything to do with football clubs

- Memorabilia from very successful bands, e.g. Beatles, Rolling Stones
- Second-hand sports equipment that is expensive to buy new
- Books that are out of print
- Photos of your wife/girlfriend in very little clothing!

Not Worth Selling

- Old CDs from your own collection (can sell for as little as 10p)
- Single items of clothing from high street shops like M&S and New Look (instead sell several bits together as a bundle)
- Old technology like PlayStation 1, Game Boys and old televisions
- Quality furniture that is neither antique nor very modern – it rarely realises its worth
- Memorabilia from defunct teen bands, e.g. Spice Girls, HearSay
- Anything that is dirty or badly damaged
- Pornographic photos of your wife/girlfriend (it's against eBay's rules)

With all the items I have listed as not worth selling there is one exception to the rule. If you want to get rid of something and are genuinely more interested in giving it a new home rather than making a bit of cash, stick it on eBay and offer it for free if the buyer collects. I have rehomed ironing boards, food processors and televisions by doing exactly this. It might seem like a lot of effort for no reward, but it's truly appalling what we dump in landfills, so do your bit for the environment and make someone's day too!

People Watching

You'll be able to get some idea of the popularity of your auction by monitoring the number of people who are watching it. To see this go to My eBay, scroll down the page to where 'Items For Sale' are listed and look at the number under the column headed 'Watching'. The more people you have watching the greater the chance of a bidding frenzy. Remember, though, that some of these watchers will be your friends or rival sellers: not all will be bidders. Unfortunately you can only see how many people are watching an auction if you are the seller and not if you are trying to bid on an auction.

Fees

The system of fees on eBay can be mind-boggling for a beginner and downright confusing for an expert. The only people who I can imagine feeling at all comfortable working out the cost of their transactions are the type of individuals who relish the prospect of completing their annual tax return… and they are pretty few and far between!

Weird & Wonderful eBay Sales

British Prime Minister's wife Cherie Blair hit the headlines when it was revealed she had bought a second-hand alarm clock for her toddler son Leo on eBay.

However, before you skip off to another chapter, I have some good news. As long as you have a basic understanding of roughly how much eBay charges and for what, fees need never trouble you again: eBay works them out, bills you and will even take the money straight from your account. No maths required!

To give you an idea of how the fees work, they can be best thought of in three separate categories: **insertion fees**, **listing extras** and **final value fees**.

Insertion Fees

Best thought of as the cost you pay to advertise on eBay, this is a basic fee that everyone pays to list their item, the cost varying depending on your starting price. You pay this fee whether your item sells or not.

Starting or Reserve Price	Insertion Fee
£0.01–£0.99	15p
£1.00–£4.99	20p
£5.00–£14.99	35p
£15.00–£29.99	75p
£30.00–£99.99	£1.50
£100 and up	£2.00

One thing that many first-timers fail to realise is that deducting 1p from your starting price can make a big difference to your insertion fee. For instance listing an item with a starting price of £30 will cost you £1.50, but if you reduce the starting price to £29.99 you will save yourself 75p!

With that knowledge it is easy to understand why so many items on eBay aren't listed with a round starting price. Sellers aren't just trying to copy the high street practice of making an item look

Facts & Figures

There are 13,000 categories on eBay.

cheaper, they are also saving themselves money on the listing fee.

Listing Extras

There are numerous extra features you can choose to add to your listing which vary in price from a few pence to £50. All are optional. For more details, refer to the 'Extra Features' chapter.

Final Value Fees

When an item sells at auction, eBay take a cut of the price it realises. Here the similarities to the British tax system come into play. There's a sliding scale of percentages based on the closing bid price.

Highest Bid	Value Fee
£0.01–£29.99	5.25%
£30.00–£599.99	5.25% on the first £29.99 plus 3.25% on the rest
Over £600	5.25% on the first £29.99 plus 3.25% up to £600 plus 1.75% on the rest

There are two exceptions to the regular fees: these are real estate and motors.

eBay Real Estate

There is a simple one-off £35.00 insertion fee for listing a property on eBay and there is no final value fee.

eBay Motors

If you sell a car, commercial vehicle, motorcycle or caravan on eBay you pay the fees for eBay Motors. These consist of a fixed insertion fee, a final value fee and fees for any optional extras.

Insertion Fee for Motors

The insertion fee for motors (£6.00 per vehicle) is much simpler than the rest of eBay. It is the same regardless of whether you list the vehicle at a fixed 'Buy It Now' price or in an auction and regardless of your starting price.

Final Value Fee for Motors

End Price	Final Value Fee
£0.01–£1,999.99	£15.00
£2,000.00–£3,999.99	0.75%
£4,000 and above	£30.00

Extras for Motors

As regular eBay.co.uk except…
Reserve price fee £3.00

How to Pay Your Fees

eBay requires payment each month on accounts that have run up fees of £1.00 or greater.
You can pay your seller fees monthly or with one-off payments either by credit card, PayPal or via direct debit straight from your bank account.

Your payment will be automatically processed if you provide eBay with your credit card details or fill in a direct debit mandate. The main advantage of choosing this automatic payment method is that eBay will not curb your selling activity. It's eBay policy that unless you have a credit card on file or a direct debit set up you will only be allowed to accrue fees of up to £15. Once that limit has been

Facts & Figures

Britons spend more time on eBay than on any other online site.

reached you need to clear your debt before you can list anything else.

If you choose to pay monthly by credit card your card will be charged 7–10 days after you receive your invoice; this will either be the fifteenth of the month or the last day of the month. If you pay by direct debit and your bank declines the charge you'll have to pay a £5.00 administration fee.

You can change your payment method or make a one-off payment ahead of your automatic payment at any time. To do this, go to My eBay. Click on 'Seller Account' which you'll find on the left-hand side, under 'My Account'. You'll then see a summary of your account activity and any outstanding fees. There are a couple of text links at the bottom of the page which will link you to areas of the site where you can change your payment method or choose a different method for one-off payment.

Writing Your Description

Title

The words you choose to use in your auction title are incredibly important. As I've mentioned already, the basic search facility on eBay (which is all that many people use) only checks titles, not descriptions, for keywords, so you have to make sure that you choose the words in your title well. Think carefully about the words that someone searching for the item you are selling would type

---

Weird & Wonderful eBay Sales

An eBay user once sold an air guitar on the site and charged £5 for postage.

---

into the search box. You are allowed 55 characters for your title including spaces and punctuation. If you find you've got some to spare when you've finished you haven't done the job properly!

Important things to include in a title are:

- The brand name
- What it is
- Size
- The word 'new' if it is
- Colour
- Model
- Age

Don't worry if your title isn't a perfect sentence – the object is to attract buyers to your auction, not to score points in an English exam!

Here are a couple of examples of how to write a good title, starting with:

Black Monsoon ball/prom/evening dress. Size 12/40

Using several words to describe the dress will increase your chances of people finding your auction. Although 'prom', 'ball' and 'evening' dresses are essentially the same thing, many people will only search for one of the words and not all of them. Likewise a UK size 12 is a European size 40. Including both increases your chances of being found by both a British and a European buyer.

NEW Little Britain DVD Region 2/UK Comedy

It sounds obvious now, but many people get so caught up in describing their item that they forget to include the most important information – what it actually is! You may have chosen to list this item under the DVD section on the site, but include the phrase in the title too – that way people who search for 'DVD' will find you as well.

Although the word 'Comedy' at the end of this title may look out of place, you have enough characters spare to add it and by doing so you may attract people who decide to search for a 'Comedy DVD'. Providing you have the space, you could also add

Weird & Wonderful eBay Sales

The skeleton of a 50,000-year-old mammoth, sold for £61,000.

the name of one of the characters in the show or of the comedians who star in it. Someone who isn't familiar with the programme might have heard of Vicky Pollard without knowing the name of the show the character is in.

Description

Unlike the title, your description has no limit on the number of characters you can use. Don't be mean with the length of your description. Failing to add information that seems obvious to you may result in people making assumptions about the item you are selling and either choosing not to bid because of this or bidding and then being disappointed with what they win.

Important information to include in your description:

Everything already in the title – some people skim-read titles and move on to descriptions, so don't worry about repeating yourself. Your title should contain the most important information about your product, so it bears repeating.

Why you are selling the item – obviously because you don't want it any more. But if you have a valid reason for getting rid of something potential buyers feel happier bidding. Reasons for selling may include needing the space, having recently bought a newer model, needing the money, moving or because you have a new hobby.

The size of the item – include all the measurements you can, even if they are only approximate. Even with clothing that has a size on its tag, it is useful to add the exact dimensions of the garment.

Its condition – if something genuinely has never been used, list it as new. If it's new and still in the original packaging include that detail. If you've worn it a couple of times, add that detail: don't simply say 'second hand' or 'used'. Basically, give as much information as you can. Being accurate and

Facts & Figures

eBay.co.uk accounts
for 10% of all of the
time UK users spend
on the Internet.

honest is what is most important, so if something is scratched or ripped mention it – potential buyers may still want to buy it.

Its history – if it's rare or collectable and there's a story behind how you acquired it, include this. A good story will encourage people to trust that your goods are genuine.

Colour – you're probably wondering why you need to include this if you have a photo. Objects look different colours in different lights, some computer screens may show a picture in a different hue, and if you spell out the colour your buyer won't be able to come back to you after they win the auction and tell you they no longer want it because it looked a different colour in the photo.

Good old-fashioned sales pitch – go crazy! Tell them how wonderful your item is, how fantastic the quality is, that you've never seen one before in such good condition, how much you have enjoyed owning it and how loath you'll be to part with it. We're all suckers for a good sales pitch!

Photographs

Photos are incredibly important when it comes to selling something on eBay. I would even go so far as to say don't bother listing without one.

In most cases it is far better to wait until you have access to a camera than to sell your goods at a lower price. Of course, the very reason that a lot of people start selling on eBay is because they are short of cash and so as a beginner I'm not

Facts & Figures

Britons spend more time on eBay than on any other online site.

suggesting you go out and spend a large sum on a digital camera purely for using on your auctions. There are, fortunately, many ways to get pictures online!

The Zero Budget Option

If you've got no money to spend on a camera, use a mobile phone. Lots of phones these days have cameras. If yours doesn't, ask round your friends and family (particularly any teenage relatives!) or talk to your service provider. If you've been on a contract for a while, you may find that you are entitled to a free upgrade to a phone with a camera.

The pictures mobile phones produce are not top quality but they do have the advantage of being very easy to transfer to the Internet. Most phones will let you send a photo direct to your e-mail address – just use the keys to type in an e-mail address rather than a phone number. To use this facility, you may need to enable your phone for

Weird & Wonderful eBay Sales

Christina Aguilera's thong and a tub of her dirty bath water sold for £810.

MMS (photo messaging). Consult your service provider.

Only Got a Tenner

These days you can buy a disposable camera for around £5. In fact, they are so cheap to produce, you'll often find they are given away as promotional gifts or as cover-mounts on magazines.

Use the camera to take photos of everything you are planning to sell. Make sure you get a couple of shots of each item just in case. Then take your camera to be developed and request a Kodak photo CD.

You can put the CD into the CD slot in your computer and select the photos direct from the disc.

Less Than £50 to Spend

If you can't afford a new digital camera, buy a second-hand one. Many of the popular models are being updated every year and old models are quickly becoming obsolete.

The Canon Ixus, which is one of the world's most popular digital cameras, has been updated six times since it launched nine years ago, with the last three models having been released in as many years. My father still uses one of the early models and apart from some minor issues with battery life he's very happy with it. The photos are perfectly adequate for all but photographic purists and crucially you have all the advantages of digital. You can see what your photo looks like immediately and the camera uploads directly to your computer.

A new model will set you back nearly £300; a second-hand early model (I suggest Ixus 200 or 300) may cost as little as £20. The higher the model number, the more recent the issue. Where can you buy a second-hand digital camera? eBay of course! Buying one on the site before you start selling will also get you some much needed feedback.

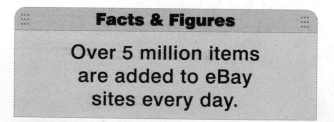

Facts & Figures

Over 5 million items are added to eBay sites every day.

One word of warning: if you do bid, ensure that you are buying a digital Ixus and not the APS Ixus, which – although it sounds similar – is a film camera.

Serious Money to Spend

I know what you're thinking – selling things on eBay could prove to be a marvellous excuse to buy a new camera. After all, it may well pay for itself in a few weeks. If you want to splash some cash on some new photographic equipment talk to a good camera retailer and read reviews online before you buy. You don't need any special features to be able to use it for eBay, but do opt for digital over film.

Other Sources For Photos

Now just in case you are thinking of 'borrowing' a photograph of your item from another auction,

Weird & Wonderful eBay Sales

A bachelor from West Sussex decided against turning up at his office Christmas party alone and sold the 'plus one' portion of his ticket on the site for £79.

let's clear that one up right away. You can't do it. It's against eBay rules. Even if the item is exactly the same as the one you are selling, you didn't take the photograph and using it in your auction is copyright theft.

Lots of people spend a great deal of time taking good pictures for their auctions and they'll be pretty annoyed if you come along and steal their work with a click of a mouse!

Aside from that point, buyers aren't daft – if you use a photo that has been or still is being used on another auction, they'll be pretty suspicious about what you are selling and wonder if you're trying to hide something about what it looks like. I refer to the comment I made at the start of this chapter: if you haven't got a photo of it, don't bother listing it.

Occasionally you yourself may become the victim of photo theft. It happened to me when I was selling an Ikea sofa. After my auction finished, someone else listed their own sofa with the photograph of mine and included in the description the line

'This isn't a photograph of our sofa, but it looks similar'.

If this happens to you, e-mail the seller first and try asking them to remove your photo. Often they'll be so embarrassed that they've been caught in the act that they'll remove it without any further action, but if they don't reply or they refuse to remove it, you can report them to eBay, who will probably cancel the auction. To report them to eBay use this link:

http://pages.ebay.co.uk/help/basics/select-support.html

Technically using stock photos of books or CDs in an auction is also copyright theft, but it's harder to prove the book or album cover in the photo isn't a photo of your own cover, so it goes on a lot more and both eBay and the publishers tend to turn a blind eye to it.

Taking Good Photos

Don't underestimate the importance of a good neutral background. I once saw a lady selling beautiful crocheted white cot covers displayed on her 1970s brown swirly carpet – and she wondered why they weren't selling!

Most houses have good surfaces to display items on. White sheets are excellent, just make sure it's flat and ironed. An unconventional approach is to put your item in a bath, it reflects the light and provides a good clear background. Hang clothing on hangers from doors or on picture hooks against a white wall.

Cropping and Rotating

Make sure you spend a little bit of time cropping your photos to cut out your feet, the family dog or anything else that isn't part of the auction. Rotating your photo where necessary is also very important – you're expecting a little too much if your potential buyers have to angle their head 90 degrees to see what you are selling!

eBay has some basic photo editing software that you can download for free once and then use as part of the listing process every time you add a photo to the site. Increasingly new computers include photo editing software as part of the software bundle, but if you do want to invest in a package try Jasc PaintShop Pro which you can pick up second-hand for about £40. This will allow you to adjust colours, lighten, rotate and crop your photos before you add them to the auction.

Displaying Clothing

If you plan to sell a lot of clothing on eBay you may want to consider investing in a mannequin or tailor's dummy to display your clothes. For one thing, if you live alone, it's extremely difficult to take photos of yourself wearing the item and even if you just list a photo of the garment on the hanger, you'll often get a request from someone to see a photo of it being worn. Don't buy a mannequin on eBay, though; the competition forces the prices sky high. There are cheaper places to get them elsewhere on the web.

Facts & Figures

eBay founder Pierre Omidyar is worth $10.4 billion and is America's sixteenth richest man.

As Many Photos as You Want For Free!

Here's a great tip for the more advanced eBayer. It is possible and perfectly legal to have as many photos as you want on your auction for free.

Upload your photos to your own web space (many ISPs provide web space as part of your package). Then call up the website on your browser.

Point your mouse at the photo and right-click. Select 'Properties' and next to 'Address' you will see the location of your photograph.

Then, when you are writing your auction description, click on the eBay tab that says 'Add your own HTML'.

Add the following code to your description in the spot where you want your photograph to appear: <IMG SRC='address'> replacing the word 'address' with the address you found by pointing

Weird & Wonderful eBay Sales

Bryan Adams' dirty socks fetched £551.

your mouse at the photograph earlier. The end result should look something like this:

<IMG SRC='http://www.blahblah.com/photos/myphoto.jpcg'>

As you are now playing around with HTML you might also want to use these tags in your description...

<P> Adding this at the end of a paragraph acts like a return key, adding a line space between the paragraph you typed and the next block of writing.

<P ALIGN> As above but the next paragraph or photo will be centred.

If all that sounds a bit too scary, try www.photobucket.com. They'll host the photos for you and they have a comprehensive tutorial explaining how to get the pictures into your auction. It's very simple, I promise!

Choosing Your Price

The first thing to do when choosing the price to list your item at is to research the market. It's easy to do. Search eBay for the item you plan to sell. It's not enough simply to look at the price next to the listing; take into account the following:

The number of items like yours currently for sale on eBay and the number of bids they have
Are there lots of items the same as yours for sale? How many of them actually have bids? Is there only one that people appear to be fighting over?

The current highest bid and the length of the time the auction has left to run

If you want to start your auction now and can't be bothered to wait to find out the end price an item reaches, its current price in the context of how long the auction has left to run will at least give you a rough idea of how much your item might fetch.

eBay is strange – things aren't always worth what you think. Sometimes they are worth a lot more, sometimes they are worth less and on some occasions it simply isn't worth listing them at all.

Armed with some idea of what you might expect to sell your item for, the next question to ask yourself is what is the minimum you would accept for the item. Don't get carried away, I'm not asking

---

Weird & Wonderful eBay Sales

If you were one of the lucky few to get hold of an Xbox 360 when they were first issued you could have made a healthy profit of at least $300 by selling it on eBay – one desperate gamer paid $5,999 for the console.

how much you hope to sell it for or how much you think it's worth. I'm asking you to consider the absolute minimum for which you would be willing to part with it. When you have that answer, you have your starting price. eBay does allow you to add a reserve price to listings, but I would advise against it. It costs extra, puts off bidders and will only result in a deluge of e-mails from potential buyers asking what your reserve is. Better to be more transparent and simply start the bidding at the minimum you are willing to accept.

If you've something good to sell, chances are it will sell for a lot more than your starting bid anyway. Moreover, if the price you list it for is lower than the final selling price of similar items currently on the site, you have an extra reason to feel confident about making the sale.

Buy It Now

This option allows you either to state that purchasers can only buy your item at a fixed price, or to list it with a Buy It Now facility *in addition* to an auction starting price. In the case of the latter option, purchasers can decide whether to try their luck at bidding or to buy the item straight away at a fixed price.

If you choose the second option, the Buy It Now price will automatically disappear from your auction as soon as someone places an opening bid. Otherwise you could end up inadvertently selling an item twice – once at auction and once at Buy It Now.

Buy It Now is useful for selling multiple identical items. All you have to do is complete the listing form including details of how many you have for sale. The item will remain listed until the relevant number of eBayers have clicked on the Buy It Now button to buy your goods.

Is it worth using Buy It Now? Certainly it is if you are sure how much you want to get for your item. As an example, if you bought a DVD player

Facts & Figures

An item of women's clothing sells every 7 seconds on eBay.

for £100 and are unable to return it to the store, you might want to list it for two prices; a starting bid of the minimum you are willing to accept for it and a Buy It Now price of £100. The advantage then is that you might find a buyer who's after that model but doesn't want to wait until the end of your auction.

If you do choose to add Buy It Now to an auction, it's worth making it significantly higher than your starting price, not just a few pence. Purchasers usually expect to pay a premium to get their goods immediately rather than waiting until the end of the auction.

Facts & Figures

eBay employs 5,700 people.

How Long to List

There are four choices of auction duration.

One day – most things that are auctioned for one day tend to be a bit suspect. They are usually listed for a day because the seller wants to sell them before eBay finds the auction and cancels it! I wouldn't advise that you list anything for this length of time. For one thing, you won't give eBay users enough of a chance to find your auction before it ends.

Three days – I would advise that you list for three days only if you have a personal deadline looming. For instance you need to sell within the week because you are moving house, need the cash or have another buyer lined up who will take the goods if you can't better the price.

Seven days – the most popular length of auction. The obvious advantages being that your auction will finish at the same time and same day as it started and that it will be visible on the site for every day of the week, so if your potential buyer only accesses the site on one day of the week they'll still have a chance to see it.

Ten days – most people use the ten day duration so that their auction spans two weekends. This is useful if you are selling something like a car that buyers may want to view before they bid. They might find your auction one weekend and view the car the next. However, it's worth noting that I've tried ten-day auctions on many occasions and, despite the increased duration of exposure on eBay, they don't seem to lead to an increase in the price that your item eventually sells for.

Weird & Wonderful eBay Sales

The original 1920s Hollywood sign that had been in storage since the late 70s was sold on eBay for $300,000.

Extra Features

I imagine there must be a whiz kid working at the eBay headquarters whose job it is to come up with new and exciting listing extras for the website. These extras are one of eBay's best sources of income but as you will learn most are entirely surplus to your requirements. You can't blame them for trying, though!

Subtitle (30p)

Only really worth using if you want to add details about where an item has to be collected from, such as 'Buyer must collect from south London, near Clapham'. Using it for this purpose might attract the attention of people who live nearby and may save you answering lots of e-mails from people asking where the item is located. Otherwise it won't give you any particular advantage. Most of the basic information about an item can be fitted into the title and anything else should be in the description. A subtitle is treated as part of the item description on the search facility so the contents of it won't be found by anyone searching titles only.

Reserve Price (fee varies)

A reserve price is the minimum price a seller will accept for an item and is usually higher than the minimum bid. If you choose this option, you will only have to sell your item to a bidder whose bid exceeds your reserve.

Facts & Figures

15,000 companies sell different software applications designed to assist with buying or selling on eBay.

As I've touched on already, most people would agree that using this tends to put people off bidding and it's pretty pointless too – all that happens is people will e-mail you asking what the reserve is! Cheaper and more straightforward would be to simply start the bidding on your item at the minimum you would be willing to accept for it.

Schedule Start Time (6p)

Worth using if your free time (i.e. when you'll be able to set up a listing) tends to be at hours of the day when eBay is quiet. It allows you to prepare your auction in advance and let eBay start the listing at a time that suits you. I spend most of my time on eBay in the morning and there are more people on eBay in the evenings, so I use this feature quite a lot. Of course, if you want to save the 6p cost, you can select this option, then go on to My eBay just before your scheduled start time and edit the auction to change the option to 'Start when submitted', but for the sake of a few pennies it's probably worth just paying the money!

Extra Pictures (12p)

The first photo for your auction is free, but you can choose to add up to 11 extra pictures at 12p a time. If you are selling a high value item, extra photos are well worth paying for, but don't go overboard. Many eBay users are still on dial-up connections and if a page takes too long to load they may give up on your auction and hit the 'Back' button. Stick to a maximum of four photos – you can always add a line of text to your description, letting potential buyers know that more photos are available on request by e-mail.

NB – Check out the 'Photographs' chapter to find out how to add as many pictures as you like to your auction for free.

Gallery (20p)

I use this option on almost every auction I list on eBay. It's the one feature that's really worth spending money on. Selecting 'Gallery' means that eBay will display a small version of your first photo in the listing of search results, allowing potential buyers to see your item before they click on the title to view your auction. It gives you a huge advantage over other sellers who don't use this option.

Gallery Featured (£15.95)

It really does cost a whopping £15.95 extra to use this feature. So what do you get for your money? By choosing this, a large version of your photo will appear (on rotation with others who have selected this option) in a special featured section at the top of the picture gallery. However, the only people who will benefit from your extravagance are the ones who choose the 'Picture Gallery' option to view their search results. You can see this option just above your first item in your list of search results.

Supersize Pictures (60p)

Allows potential buyers to see extra large versions of your photos. Useful if you are selling something where small details of the item are important, such as clothes or antiques.

Picture Show (15p)

The whiz-kid who invents the extra features on eBay only recently came up with this and presumably got him- or herself a nice bonus in the process. Scared your punters will run off before they scroll down to the bottom of the page? This facility allows you to bombard them with a slide show of several photos in place of the usual solo one at the top of the page.

Picture Pack (90p for up to 6 pictures or £1.35 for 7–12 pictures)

A veritable Christmas stocking of features for one price. This option gives you gallery, supersize, picture show and additional pictures for one price. Good value for money if you're selling something that you need to show a lot of photos of.

Listing Designer (7p)

The listing designer is a patterned background that you can decorate your auction with. Designs vary to match the item you are selling. I hang my head in shame as I admit to you that I used to use this feature when I first sold on eBay. Listing designers are to eBay auctions what artex ceilings are to houses. If the item you are selling is really so dull that you need to liven it up with a border of animal prints or pastel-coloured baby rattles, you shouldn't waste your time listing it. Step away from the listing designer, there's nothing to see.

Bold (75p)

Displays the title of your auction in bold when search results are displayed. I'm not convinced it attracts significantly more attention to your auction.

Highlight (£2.50)

Highlights your auction details with a coloured band on search results. Expensive for what it is.

Featured Category Auction (£9.95)

Your auction will appear in a special section at the top of the page when it comes up in a search, regardless of how a user chooses to sort the results. Your auction will also appear under featured items in the category list you choose for the item.

Home Page Featured (£49.95)

Choosing this feature will mean that your item appears on the main page of www.ebay.co.uk under 'Featured Items'. Useful if you are selling something either ridiculously expensive, amazingly unique or both. I'm thinking Margaret Thatcher's handbag or Britney Spears' bra here. Though as the rules for this category prohibit using it for

'Listings for novelty items and other items in poor taste', with the two examples I just quoted you might come unstuck! It's worth pointing out that if you choose this option your auction will appear on rotation with others that have chosen this option and you will only be featured on the front page of the British site ebay.co.uk.

Buy It Now (fee varies)

If you want to create the option for potential buyers to purchase your item at a fixed price, there is a small charge on a sliding scale.

Buy It Now price of £0.01–£4.99	5p
Buy It Now price of £5.00–£14.99	10p
Buy It Now price of £15.00–£29.99	15p
Buy It Now price of £30.00 or more	25p

Facts & Figures

The most expensive item ever sold on eBay was a Gulf-stream jet, which sold for $4.9m (£2.57m).

Postage

Once you have completed the description of your item and decided on your price, you'll be asked to specify postage costs.

This is where a lot of first-time sellers run into difficulty – I'll never forget sending one item I had sold where the postage ended up costing more than the total sum I received from the sale and my quoted postage charge combined. In other words, it actually cost me money to give my goods away!

There will probably be a few things you decide to sell on eBay that you will think you won't be able to post because they are too big or too heavy. With the exception of the obvious items (cars, conservatories, sofas…) almost everything can be sent through the post.

The big advantage to providing a postal price for a large item is that you will immediately open up your market, not just to people who live far away but also to potential buyers who don't have cars or can't be bothered to collect it.

You can, of course, choose to list your item without adding a specified postage cost, but it will discourage some eBay users and others will just e-mail you and ask how much it will be. So sooner or later you're going to have to find out how much your goods will cost to send.

If the thought of trudging to the post office twice with your entire record collection is suddenly

Weird & Wonderful eBay Sales

A businessman was conned out of $802,600 by a joker who 'sold' him the Indian Prime Minister's house in an eBay auction. The scam only came to light when the new owner turned up to take possession of the house.

putting you off the idea of selling it, don't panic!
You can find out how much it will cost to send
most items by using a set of kitchen scales and
the Royal Mail website.

Weigh your goods and the packaging you intend
to send them in, take a note of the combined
weight and log on to www.royalmail.com. Here
you can find postage costs for first and second
class as well as airmail and international post.
Once you have a price, remember to add on
enough to cover the costs of your packaging and
handling. Handling is a grey area and loosely
covers travel expenses and time taken to wrap the
package and drive to the post office.

Don't get carried away, though. Adding the bus
fare to the post office is fine, but not the new coat

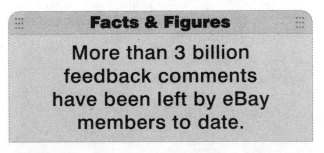

Facts & Figures

More than 3 billion
feedback comments
have been left by eBay
members to date.

you bought to go there! Most people agree that it is acceptable to make a small profit on postage, but if you make the price too high people may not bid.

The other down side to charging high postage costs is that there are actually people who check the value of the stamps you've put on the package against the charge you made for postage and get quite cross if there is a difference. Fortunately they are relatively few and far between, but it's worth knowing people like that do exist so you can be prepared for disputes or negative feedback.

You will find as you sell more and more on eBay that you'll begin to learn what postage costs to specify for certain goods. The following is a list of some items commonly sold on eBay and the amount I would include in the auction information for first-class postage costs within the UK. Postage itself is likely to be a fair bit less than the sum I would quote.

Weird & Wonderful eBay Sales

Joanna Lumley's Ferrari was sold on eBay for £35,000.

Postcard or tickets	70p
CD	£1.20
Item of children's clothing	£1.50
Video or DVD	£2.00
T-shirt	£2.00
Jeans	£3.00
Shoes	£5.00
Video camera	£10

You can also, of course, get a good idea of how much to charge for postage by checking the p. & p. listed on similar auctions. If you are selling something unusual and you find someone else who is selling the same thing, there's no harm in e-mailing them after an auction has ended to see what the exact

Facts & Figures

Meg Whitman, eBay's boss since 1998, has shareholdings worth more than £850m.

costs were. eBay is a pretty friendly place and most people are happy to help when they can.

There'll be some items that you are able to send in the post but which are so large or heavy that you'd find it difficult to weigh them at home. With this scenario, don't give up and simply list them as 'Will arrange local pickup (no postage)'. By adding a postage option you are likely to increase the final price you sell for significantly, so it's worth the gamble of guessing the postage and being prepared to swallow the extra cost if you are wrong. You'd be surprised how reasonable postage of large parcels is. The most I have ever been quoted to mail an item was £24, which was the cost to send two extremely heavy professional record decks and a mixer.

So, what happens if after the auction has ended you discover that postage will be more expensive than you expected?

Weird & Wonderful eBay Sales

Britney Spears' chewed and spat-out chewing gum reached £270.

The good news is that eBay rules state you are allowed to 'reasonably increase postage costs'. If you need to do this, send an e-mail explaining the problem clearly and honestly to the buyer and don't try and force them to pay. If they feel like they are being made to pay more than they bargained for, they may leave negative feedback. Often it's worth paying the extra cost yourself and learning the lesson for next time.

Another question you may get asked is whether you will insure the parcel. If you are selling small value items, a Certificate of Posting – which is free at post offices – will insure goods worth up to £28. Speak nicely to the person in the post office and they may even give you a pad of them so you can complete them in advance.

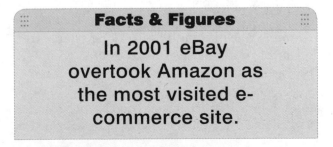

Facts & Figures

In 2001 eBay overtook Amazon as the most visited e-commerce site.

For higher value items insurance can be obtained for a small cost. It's a good investment and it makes sense to include it in your p. & p. costs, rather than letting your purchaser decide whether or not they want to pay for it. The careful, belt and braces approach will save you hassles in the long run.

It's a good idea to include details of when you are likely to post your item in your description. Most bidders expect a package to be dispatched within a couple of days, so if you only go to the post office once a week, make sure you spell that out to avoid getting an unhappy buyer.

Sending Internationally

Opening up your market to international buyers is very easy (it just involves ticking a box when you list your item) and is another way to get the best price for your goods.

A simple rule of thumb for working out the cost of international postage is to double your UK postage costs.

Remember eBay has an approved list of countries to mail to. Unfortunately transactions with buyers in African countries are more often than not problematic; be on your guard particularly for requests to mail to Nigeria. (For more information see the chapter called 'Scams'.)

Packaging

When you begin selling on eBay you'll probably purchase Jiffy bags one by one from a local shop, but this is by far the most expensive way to buy your packaging and if you begin to sell regularly it's handy to have a stash at home. Conveniently, you can buy all your packaging on eBay and get some feedback to increase your rating while you are at it! Simply search for the word 'packaging' or head to 'Buy' and look under Business, Office and Industrial > Packing and Posting Supplies, where you'll find thousands of auctions selling envelopes, tape, boxes and postage scales.

Some of the most popular packaging includes:

- **Plastic mailers** – come in a variety of sizes with self-sealing closure
- **Packaging tape** – thicker, stronger and less fiddly than ordinary Sellotape

- **Jiffy bags** – use only when something is solid or fragile: sending soft things like clothing in Jiffys just adds cost
- **Bubble wrap** – great for larger items and can be wrapped round smaller items and used with plastic mailers as a substitute for Jiffy bags
- **Brown paper** – useful for irregular shaped or larger items

You'll usually find auctions selling a range of specialist boxes for jewellery, watches and craft gifts.

Although you might hesitate over buying your packaging bulk, you'll be amazed how quickly you get through it once you have been bitten by the eBay bug.

Weird & Wonderful eBay Sales

The plaster cast from Wayne Rooney's broken foot went for £2,000.

Buyers' Questions

You'll find with most auctions that no matter how hard you try to include all the information about your item, potential bidders will still have questions. These will be sent via eBay to your own e-mail account and a copy will also be available in your eBay inbox, which you can access via My eBay.

Rather than simply clicking 'Reply' on the e-mail, you can click on the link within it that says 'respond to this question'. This way, you'll be taken to a page on eBay allowing you to reply to the e-mail, and by ticking a box beneath your reply, choose to add your reply to the bottom of your auction page so that all potential bidders can see it. Ticking this box to add the information to your listing has two advantages. Firstly it will save you answering the same question from several different people, and secondly if potential bidders see that you have had questions to respond to they'll realise they aren't the only one interested in your item and may get more competitive with their bidding.

One question that you will inevitably be asked at some point is whether you will accept an offer on your item and close the auction early. I would always advise against doing this. People who make this request usually fall into two groups: either they know the true value of your item and hope to get it cheaper by making you an offer before the auction has run its course; or they are a rival seller who wants to get rid of a competing auction. If the latter is true, you are also unlikely to see any money from them.

Weird & Wonderful eBay Sales

Michelle Monroe financed her £2,500 breast enlargement operation via an eBay auction. A mystery businessman paid the sum in exchange for the right to examine them after the operation.

Unfortunately one thing I have noticed about people who ask questions is that they are very rarely the winning bidder. However, if you answer their question they may place a bid (even if it isn't the winning one) and so ultimately contribute to the final price your item reaches.

Receiving Payments

After an auction finishes you will be sent an e-mail telling you how much your item sold for. Within this e-mail will be a clickable link which will take you to the section of eBay where you can send out invoices.

Many purchasers will make their payments instantly; some will take several days; others won't realise that they should inform you they are sending a cheque and you'll only discover that they are when it turns up. Most people will pay within a week, so don't be concerned if you hear nothing for a few days – some people can only access the site at work and others will be waiting for pay day.

Cash on Collection

Don't be embarrassed to count it or to hold it up to the light to check the watermark. For a high value item I find it's useful to have a friend with me to do the counting. Whilst they are doing that I can write a receipt and sort out anything I need to organise before the handover.

PayPal

When someone makes a payment to your PayPal account you'll be notified by e-mail. Once the money is in your account you can withdraw it and transfer it to your bank account. There is a small charge for transfers of less than £50. Those over £50 are free. Log into your account and click on the 'Withdraw' tab at the top of the page. Of course you don't have to withdraw it; you can just leave the money in your PayPal account and use it to pay for things when you make purchases on eBay.

Cheques

If they are for a sum over £10 wait for them to clear before you send out the item. Clearing time varies, but allow approximately ten days and if you are in any doubt check it has cleared by talking to the bank before you send the item. If the cheque is for less than £10 send the goods straight away: this is because most banks charge £10 if a cheque bounces, so a cheque for less than that sum is very unlikely to bounce.

Postal Orders

Sign them and take them to the post office where they will be exchanged for cash.

Escrow

Buyer and seller agree terms, the buyer pays an escrow service, the seller sends the item and once the buyer has inspected the goods and is happy with them he informs the escrow service who release the money to the buyer.

Bank Deposit

Bank transfers are often instant if the two parties are with the same bank, but can take up to a week between different banks. Wait until you have confirmation the money has reached you before you send out the auction item.

Banker's Draft

Take it to your bank where it is cashed like a cheque. There is no need to wait for the money to clear.

PART FOUR: APPENDIX

Top 10 Do's and Don'ts

Do

 make the effort to take a good photograph get a Certificate of Posting for everything you send

 make sure you have packaging organised before you list an item. A week goes very quickly!

 answer questions promptly

 look elsewhere on the Internet for your item to make sure eBay is offering the item you want at the best price

- assume that any auction that looks too good to be true probably is

- leave feedback for your trading partners

- believe that most people are honest and most auctions are legit

- ask for help on the eBay discussion boards say that you will send your item abroad – you'll get more bids

Don't

- ever send payment via Western Union

- leave negative feedback before giving the seller a chance to correct the problem

- waste money on unnecessary and expensive listing extras

- assume anything about an item you are bidding on: if you're not sure, ask!

- exceed your self-imposed spending limit. If you aren't the highest bidder on this auction, you'll probably get a chance to bid on something similar on another day

- lie about the item you are selling in the description

- ever respond to e-mails purporting to be from eBay or PayPal. Neither companies will ever ask for your log-in information

- respond if someone asks you to contact them directly to arrange a deal instead of completing the auction through eBay

- send an item before you've received payment

- end an auction early

- flood the market. If you have more than one item the same, only list one at a time

- buy anything from a seller whose feedback details are hidden

eBay Scams

Although eBay is on the whole a friendly and safe community, there are inevitably people who will try and use it as an opportunity to con people. Here's a brief summary of some of the most common eBay scams.

Remember, if in doubt, should you receive an e-mail claiming to be from eBay or a strange request via the site it is always advisable to check eBay's own regularly updated safety information

Facts & Figures

58% of eBay users in the UK are over 35.

which you can find at http://www.ebay.co.uk/
safetycentre.

Phishing

A popular con that is often targeted at Internet
bank users, but is also used to extract information
from eBay account holders. Victims receive an
e-mail purporting to be from eBay and typically
threatening to close your account or warning of
an attempted hack on it. Scammers are clever and
will do everything to convince you that the e-mail
is real; most likely it will include the eBay logo and
sometimes there'll even be links to the actual eBay
User Agreement and Privacy Policy.

The aim of the e-mails is always the same: to get
you to click on a link in the mail which will take
you to a website which appears to be eBay and then
get you to re-enter your account information.

Weird & Wonderful eBay Sales

American singer Jessica Simpson
bought the red cowboy boots she wore
in the video for 'These Boots are Made
for Walking' on eBay. They cost her $95
(£54).

You should be *very* suspicious of any e-mail asking you to verify your account information. eBay and PayPal will never ask for your personal or financial information in an e-mail.

Recently phishers have adopted an even more devious method of trying to get you to divulge your password. They mimic the e-mails you get from potential buyers and ask an innocent sounding question such as 'Do you accept PayPal on this auction?' The scammers bank on the fact that people will click on the 'Respond Now' button in the e-mail and type their password into the spoof eBay site it leads them to.

Facts & Figures

There are more than 724,000 professional sellers in the U.S. who use eBay as a primary or secondary source of income.

The best way to avoid falling for this trick is to check the date in any e-mails purporting to be from eBay and also look within the e-mail for details of the auction that the question refers to. If the date's not current or the auction details are missing, open your browser and go to www.ebay.co.uk. If you have any questions pending for your auctions, you'll find details in My eBay. If you don't, it was a scam.

The Overpaid Cheque Scam

After selling an item on eBay you are contacted by the winning bidder who tells you they will send you a cheque for a large sum of money (always more than their winning bid) as payment for the auction item, requesting at the same time that you write a cheque for the 'surplus' and return it to them. Cunningly they may try to claim that this method of payment ensures the item is sent as both parties are making an initial outlay.

Weird & Wonderful eBay Sales

A decommissioned nuclear bunker in Pickering, North Yorkshire was sold on eBay for £17,100.

No sooner have you sent them a cheque than you will find the original payment bounces and you are left out of pocket. The goal of the scam is the cash 'overpayment', not the goods, which are often directed to a non-existent address.

Methods of Payment

Never be persuaded to use anything other than eBay's approved methods of payment. In particular never use instant money transfer services such as Western Union or MoneyGram to pay for your eBay items. This method of payment is unsafe when paying someone you don't know.

You may also be asked to use a payment system you have never heard of. Often you'll find this is a website, not a legitimate payment service, and has instead been set up by fraudsters to extract your financial information from you.

Facts & Figures

eBay's net profits for the second quarter of 2005 were £161m.

Payment methods are always outlined in auctions by the seller. Be sure to check before you bid.

Pyramid Schemes

The scourge of the middle-class dinner party has reared its ugly head in a new form on eBay.

An auction will appear to offer a desirable product like an MP3 player, games console or mobile phone for an incredibly cheap price, sometimes as little as £10.

The potential purchaser is told not to bid on the auction, but instead is directed to a website where these goods are offered as a free gift when you buy something like a book or a CD.

Facts & Figures

11 million people currently visit the eBay.co.uk site every month.

The catch is your purchase is little more than a ticket to join the pyramid scheme. When making a purchase, the buyer's name is added to the pyramid and you only get the gift if and when enough people sign up to push you to the top of the list. To speed up the process, buyers are often encouraged to recruit new members to join the scheme.

As with all pyramid schemes, mathematical logic dictates that these pyramids always collapse because their growth is not sustainable. As the scheme grows, the number of new members needed to support it grows exponentially. The number of people needed to sustain the scheme quickly escalates until it exceeds the world's population.

Dealing Off eBay

To point out the obvious, eBay will only protect you if you carry out the transaction on their site.

Weird & Wonderful eBay Sales

A half-finished bottle of Kurt Cobain's beer sold for £175.

Do not be persuaded to carry out a purchase in any other way. Sometimes you'll see an auction that will tell you to e-mail the seller to arrange a private 'Buy It Now' deal. If you do this and negotiate a deal via e-mail you will not be covered by any of eBay's buyer protection. It doesn't matter that the original auction was listed on eBay; once you deal off eBay you are not covered. Bid in the auction, or purchase via the 'Buy It Now' button instead.

Dictionary of eBay Terms and Acronyms

eBay has several words and abbreviations that you will see appearing in auctions and the forums. To avoid being totally baffled, keep this list handy when you are next online.

Bid Shielding: Putting in a second very high bid on an auction (usually with a different user ID) with the intention of cancelling it at the last minute, so that the earlier smaller bid wins. It's pretty complex and quite rare, so no need to worry about it too much!

BIN: Buy It Now – the option on eBay that allows you to purchase an item at a fixed price rather than in an auction.

BNIB: Brand New In Box.

BNWL: Brand New With Labels.

BNWOT: Brand New Without Tags.

BNWT: Brand New With Tags.

BUMP: Use this one-word response (short for Bring Up My Post) to reply to a useful posting, as the postings with the most replies stay at the top of the discussion list.

Buyer's remorse: A common affliction suffered by buyers on eBay when they get carried away and spend more than they should in an auction. It usually results in them asking to retract their winning bid, returning the goods or sobbing over their keyboard and imposing a month long eBay ban on him- or herself!

EOA: End Of Auction.

FB: Feedback.

FVF: Final Value Fee – the fee you pay to eBay at the end of an auction based on the end price your item sells for.

Keyword Spamming: Including words in your auction title or description that don't have anything to do with the item you are auctioning, with the specific aim of increasing your chances of having your auction found in a search, e.g. 'Lovely coat. Not Next, Marks & Spencer or Jigsaw'.

LOL: Laugh Out Loud.

MIB: Mint In Box (perfect condition and in original box).

NARU: Not A Registered User – self-explanatory except for the fact that it is often used to describe someone who used to be, but is no longer a

Weird & Wonderful eBay Sales

Really stuck for ideas? One American eBay dealer sold 'nothing' on the site for $1.

registered user after being struck off by eBay, e.g. 'That troublemaker is now NARU'.

Negging: The process of leaving negative feedback.

Newbie: A person who is new to eBay.

Nibbling: Making repeated bids in small increments in an attempt to become the highest bidder in an auction. Usually a sign of an inexperienced eBayer. The series of bids can often give a competing bidder an idea of the nibbling bidder's bid increments, allowing them to snipe the novice.

NPB: Non Paying Bidder – a person who bids on an auction and doesn't come up with the cash.

NPS: Non Performing Seller – a seller who fails to send the goods after the buyer pays.

Weird & Wonderful eBay Sales

18 holes of golf with Tiger Woods were sold on eBay for £236,000.

NR: No Reserve.

OP: A term you will see used in the eBay forums – it stands for 'Original Poster' and refers to the person who started that particular thread.

Pinks/Pinkies: Officials working for eBay whose postings in the forums appear with pink headers.

Shill bidding: An illegal practice where a seller uses another account or a friend to bid on an item he is selling in order to push the price of an auction higher.

Sniping: The practice of placing a winning bid in the final few seconds of an auction and snatching the item away from a previous high bidder. Completely legal but much moaned about by people who are new to eBay and not expecting it to happen.

TOS: Terms Of Service.

Trading Assistants: eBayers who sell on behalf of other members.

Related titles from Summersdale

THE BEGINNER'S GUIDE TO
computers
AND THE internet

WINDOWS® XP EDITION!

- Word processing
- Using disks
- Managing files
- Computer games
- Using the Internet
- E-mailing

SUSAN HOLDEN
MATTHEW FRANCIS

The Beginner's Guide to Computers and the Internet

Windows® XP Edition

Susan Holden and Matthew Francis

£5.99

ISBN 1-84024-396-1
ISBN 978-1-84024-396-3

CPU, Intel, VDU, server, Megabyte, MHz, monitor, DVD...

Forget the technical jargon. This is a concise and down-to-earth guide that will help you become computer literate – in your own time and on your own terms. You can do it.

Beginning with the basics, *The Beginner's Guide to Computers and the Internet* explains, in your language, the useful terms and shortcuts that will enable you to use a computer with confidence and competence.

Includes everything you need to know to benefit from the Internet and e-mail and to get it working for you.

'Book of the month: an excellent book for cutting through all the techno-speak, and showing you the basics of getting started with a computer.'

Internet Made Easy

THE BEGINNER'S GUIDE TO

broadband

AND wireless INTERNET

 Wireless Networks

 Computer Security

 Instant Messaging

 Downloading Music

 PC Phone Calls

 Wi-Fi and Laptops

PETER BURNS

The Beginner's Guide to Broadband and Wireless Internet

Peter Burns

£5.99

ISBN 1-84024-499-2
ISBN 978-1-84024-499-1

Broadband opens up a wealth of new software and websites. This unique and invaluable handbook includes key information and guides you through the decisions you'll need to make, from choosing the right anti-virus software to setting up a wireless network in your home.

Learn how to make the most of your high-speed connection, with chapters on instant messaging, downloading music, making phone calls from your computer and finding the best broadband websites on the net. It's the book everyone with broadband needs next to their PC.

Peter Burns is the marketing manager (Internet and eCommerce) for retailer Waitrose and manages waitrose.com broadband. He is also the author of *Top 100 Internet Mistakes*.

www.summersdale.com